TATTOO JOINT

DRAMA SERIES 25

 Canada Council for the Arts   Conseil des Arts du Canada

ONTARIO ARTS COUNCIL
CONSEIL DES ARTS DE L'ONTARIO

Guernica Editions Inc. acknowledges the support of
The Canada Council for the Arts
and the Ontario Arts Council.

JASON GILENO

TATTOO JOINT

A PLAY

GUERNICA

TORONTO · BUFFALO · CHICAGO · LANCASTER (U.K.)

2005

Translation copyright © 2005, by Jason Gileno and Guernica Editions Inc.
All rights reserved. The use of any part of this publication, reproduced, transmitted in any form or by any means, electronic, mechanical, photocopying, recording or otherwise stored in a retrieval system, without the prior consent of the publisher is an infringement of the copyright law.

Antonio D'Alfonso, Editor
Guernica Editions Inc.
P.O. Box 117, Station P, Toronto (ON), Canada M5S 2S6
2250 Military Road, Tonawanda, N.Y. 14150-6000 U.S.A.

Distributors:
University of Toronto Press Distribution,
5201 Dufferin Street, Toronto, (ON), Canada M3H 5T8

Gazelle Book Services, Falcon House, Queen Square, Lancaster LA1 1RN U.K.

Independent Publishers Group,
814 N. Franklin Street, Chicago, Il. 60610 U.S.A.

First edition.
Printed in Canada.
Legal Deposit – Fourth Quarter
National Library of Canada
Library of Congress Catalog Card Number: 2005931736
Library and Archives Canada Cataloguing in Publication
Gileno, Jason
Tattoo joint / Jason Gileno.
A play.
ISBN 1-55071-213-6
I. Title.
PS8613.I425T38 2005   C812'.6   C2005-905216-3

TATTOO JOINT

ACT I

SCENE 1

Soft yellow light as if from a street lamp reveals a bus stop and bench. Cop looks left and then right. He stops and sits on the bench. Fade.

Fade in to reveal a sparsely furnished room with a bare, wooden floor, a large curtainless window. Along one wall is a stack of canned tomatoes. Upon a shelf on one wall, sits a mug, a spoon, a can opener and a jar of instant coffee. Canned tomatoes are stacked against another wall. A small grooming table sits in the corner of the room above which hangs a mirror. On the table is a hairbrush and a fishbowl. Joint sits downstage, facing the large window, staring out into the night. A gentle tap on the door is heard.

JOINT: I'm sorry, we're closed. (*Pause.*) We close at nine o'clock. (*More knocking.*) It's after nine. We close at nine. (*Pause.*) Come back tomorrow. We open at nine. (*More Knocking.*) Look, I don't want to be rude, but we closed at nine. It's after nine so there's no way that you're gettin' inside. (*Alexandra enters.*)

ALEXANDRA: The door was unlocked. (*Joint is startled.*) Sorry.

JOINT: You should be!

ALEXANDRA: Well, it looks like it might rain...

JOINT: You scared the hell outta me!

ALEXANDRA: And it's cold.

JOINT: So you just break into a place?

ALEXANDRA: The door was unlocked!

JOINT: The door was not unlocked.

ALEXANDRA: It was. I turned the handle and it opened.
JOINT: I locked it myself at nine o'clock. Because that's what time we close. At nine! That door was locked. (*Pause.*)
ALEXANDRA: I'm sorry for barging in. But, I'm cold and I'm tired and...
JOINT: Are you here for a tattoo?
ALEXANDRA: What?
JOINT: A tattoo. I assume that's why you're here?
ALEXANDRA: This is a tattoo parlour?
JOINT: It doesn't look like a tattoo parlour.
ALEXANDRA: Uh, not really.
JOINT: Well, read the sign.
ALEXANDRA: What sign?
JOINT: On the window...
ALEXANDRA: There's no sign.
JOINT: On the window?
ALEXANDRA: Or anywhere.
JOINT: That's peculiar. (*Joint moves toward the window.*) It was there.
ALEXANDRA: It's not there now.
JOINT: It's gone?
ALEXANDRA: Gone.
JOINT: Vanished?
ALEXANDRA: Disappeared.
JOINT: Well! That explains it.
ALEXANDRA: What?
JOINT: Business hasn't been booming.
ALEXANDRA: Oh?
JOINT: You're the first person to come in here in a long time.
ALEXANDRA: How long?
JOINT: Two years. So do you want a tattoo or...?
ALEXANDRA: Two years? You haven't had a customer in two years?
JOINT: It's just a lull.
ALEXANDRA: That's remarkable.
JOINT: What?

TATTOO JOINT

ALEXANDRA: You haven't had a single person walk through that door in two years... a customer or otherwise?

JOINT: And...

ALEXANDRA: And you weren't even going to let me in. *(Pause.)*

JOINT: We close at nine.

ALEXANDRA: Would you mind if I sat down? To warm up a minute? *(Alexandra moves past Joint, looking around as she does. She moves to sit in the "Tattooing Chair.")*

JOINT: Not there! That is the Tattooing Chair. That chair is only for those who are here to have a tattoo. Are you here for a tattoo? *(He waits for a response.)* Sit over there. *(Joint points to an identical wooden chair across floor. Alexandra sits. Joint stands facing her and waits. Long pause.)* Warm yet?

ALEXANDRA: I'm sorry to be such an imposition on your busy routine. If you want to send a young woman all by herself back out into the cold so badly then I'll go. Okay? I'll just fend for myself.

JOINT: Okay, goodnight.

ALEXANDRA: I was being sarcastic.

JOINT: I'll tell you what. I'll make some coffee. A quick cup and then you go. Okay?

(Joint moves toward the shelf.)

ALEXANDRA: Joint?

JOINT: Yes?

ALEXANDRA: Nothing.

JOINT: Nothing?

ALEXANDRA: Sorry.

JOINT: Sorry for what?

ALEXANDRA: Nothing.

JOINT: Sorry for nothing?

ALEXANDRA: Right. *(Pause. Joint turns back toward shelf.)* I'm Alex.

JOINT: Alex?

ALEXANDRA: Alexandra.

JOINT: Fine. *(Joint turns toward shelf.)*

ALEXANDRA: And you?
JOINT: What about me?
ALEXANDRA: Your name?
JOINT: What is it?
ALEXANDRA: Yes.
JOINT: You don't know?
ALEXANDRA: How would I?
JOINT: You said it.
ALEXANDRA: I said it?
JOINT: That's right.
ALEXANDRA: No, I didn't.
JOINT: You did.
ALEXANDRA: I didn't.
JOINT: I heard you.
ALEXANDRA: When?
JOINT: Just now.
ALEXANDRA: When?
JOINT: Just then.
ALEXANDRA: I don't think so...
JOINT: You said "Joint." I said "what?" You said "nothing."
ALEXANDRA: I... I was...
SPEAKING CLOCK: THE TIME IS NINE-FORTY-FIVE P.M. NINE-FORTY-FIVE, IS THE TIME.
ALEXANDRA: What the hell was that?
JOINT: That was my speaking clock.
ALEXANDRA: I don't see any clock.
JOINT: You're not supposed to see a speaking clock... What is so funny?
ALEXANDRA: Do you think it might be ready?
JOINT: What?
ALEXANDRA: The coffee.
JOINT: I haven't made any.
ALEXANDRA: Sorry. You said you would.
JOINT: Then I will.
ALEXANDRA: Good. (*Pause. Joint turns toward shelf.*) Do you have French Roast? I like French Roast.
JOINT: I'll check. (*Joint goes over to the shelf.*)

ALEXANDRA: French Roast reminds me of Paris.

JOINT: You've been to Paris?

ALEXANDRA: No. But Paris is the nicest place to visit. Especially in the fall. French Roast always brings back memories of Paris... *(Joint is looking on the shelf.)*

JOINT: I don't have any.

ALEXANDRA: Memories of Paris?

JOINT: French Roast.

ALEXANDRA: Oh...

JOINT: I have instant.

ALEXANDRA: Instant will be fine. With double cream and one sugar please. That's how my mother used to drink her coffee. With one sugar and two creams. Coffee with one sugar and double cream always reminds me of my mother.

JOINT: I have black.

ALEXANDRA: Black will be fine. *(Joint brings her a cup. He sits.)* Aren't you having one?

JOINT: No.

ALEXANDRA: Why not?

JOINT: I don't have another mug.

(She sips. Music begins. Fade.)

SCENE 2

Stage lights rise to street scene. Cop sitting on bench. Enter widow. She sits on the bench beside him.

WIDOW: There's no bus at this hour.
COP: I'm not waiting for the bus.
WIDOW: The last bus was at nine o'clock.
COP: I'm not waiting for the bus.
WIDOW: It's long after nine now. (*Cop nods.*) It's never on time, that bus. But it's never this late!
COP: I'm not waiting for the bus. (*Cop looks at her. At the same time, she looks away. Cop looks away. They hold that pose. Then she turns to him.*)
WIDOW: You'd have a long wait if you were. It won't be by again until tomorrow. (*Cop nods.*) Tomorrow at nine. (*They both look in opposite directions. Cop turns to her.*) I'm a widow. My husband is dead. People die every day, but you never think it's going to be one of yours.
COP: I'm sorry.
WIDOW: Don't be. He was a bastard.
  Pause.
WIDOW: He's dead now.
  Pause.
COP: How'd he die?
WIDOW: Which time?
COP: Which time?
WIDOW: The first time was a stroke. He was dead for forty-five minutes. Stone cold. And then, it was the funniest thing. He just jumped out of bed and started running like

a maniac up and down the halls of the hospital. He thought he was a medieval knight. "Where's my armour?" he screamed. "Where's my armour?"

COP: His armour?

WIDOW: That's what I said! "What armour, you dotty old loon?" But he sure wanted to find it.

COP: What for?

WIDOW: He needed it, to finish his quest.

COP: His quest?

WIDOW: That's what I said. "What quest, you dotty old loon?" Of course, his hospital gown was untied in the back, so it was a little hard to take him seriously.

COP: Ma'am, what sort of quest? (*Widow, smiling, doesn't respond.*) Ma'am, what sort of quest?

WIDOW: I don't know. I can't imagine what sort of quest that wrinkled old turnip would be on. A quest to the back of the refrigerator, maybe. Man in search of pork chop. Ha! Imagine! My husband the hero! (*Widow turns away.*) He's dead for sure, this time. (*Cop turns away.*) Nope, not saving any princesses now. (*Widow turns to Cop.*) He's buried in my front yard you know.

COP: I should be going.

WIDOW: You wanna know what his trouble was? (*Pause.*) He was in love with another woman. The bastard.

COP: Who was it?

WIDOW: She didn't have a name. She didn't even have a face! Just a nameless, faceless fantasy. But there's something very alluring about a girl without a face. You know what I mean?

(*Cop turns to her. Fade.*)

SCENE 3

Joint's Tattoo Joint.

JOINT: Let's try this another way. So, what brings you to our little town?
ALEXANDRA: I need a reason to come here?
JOINT: Well, it's a pretty small town. I mean look around. There's not much to see.
ALEXANDRA: I've seen a few things.
JOINT: Like what? There's only one road. There's a barbershop. There's a general store. And there's a big open space. We don't even have a church.
ALEXANDRA: There's a bed and breakfast.
JOINT: It's only got one bed! It's bungalow, owned by a lonely widow who rents out her living room whenever someone visits here. But –
ALEXANDRA: But what?
JOINT: No one ever visits here.
ALEXANDRA: How did you wind up here?
JOINT: There are two ways that people wind up in a town like this. One is you're born here, in which case you spend the great majority of your time looking for ways to leave. The other is escape.
ALEXANDRA: Escape?
JOINT: Running from something.
ALEXANDRA: Which one are you?
JOINT: I wasn't born here.
ALEXANDRA: Then what are you running from? (*Joint doesn't answer.*) Peter? (*Pause.*)

JOINT: What?
ALEXANDRA: What are you running from?
JOINT: Who's Peter?
ALEXANDRA: What? (*Joint begins to feed fish.*)
JOINT: You just called me Peter.
ALEXANDRA: I did?
JOINT: Yeah.
ALEXANDRA: When?
JOINT: Just then.
ALEXANDRA: I don't think so.
JOINT: You said "what are you running from?" I said nothing. You said "Peter…"
SPEAKING CLOCK: THE TIME IS TEN-FIFTEEN P.M. TEN-FIFTEEN IS THE TIME.
JOINT (*To fish*): Somebody's not telling all there is to tell, Apollo. (*Joint listens.*) Apollo thinks you're full of shit too.
ALEXANDRA: He does, does he? (*Alexandra goes over to fish bowl.*) Oh my.
JOINT: What?
ALEXANDRA: I don't think Apollo's feeling so well.
JOINT: He's fine.
ALEXANDRA: I think he might be dead.
JOINT: He's fine.
ALEXANDRA: No, he's dead.
JOINT: He's just shy.
ALEXANDRA: He's floating.
JOINT: He's not a morning person.
ALEXANDRA: It's ten o'clock at night…
JOINT: …I thought we were talking about you?
ALEXANDRA: Were we?
JOINT: You were about to tell me the truth, I think.
ALEXANDRA: The truth?
JOINT: Why you're here.
ALEXANDRA: You're right.
JOINT: Of course I'm right.
ALEXANDRA: There is another reason I'm here…
JOINT: Of course there is.

ALEXANDRA: I came here to get a tattoo.
JOINT: That's right, you came here to get a... Wait. Really?
ALEXANDRA: Yes.
JOINT: That changes everything. Sorry. Two years without a customer. One gets a little crotchety. Come sit in the chair and we'll get started.
ALEXANDRA: Uhh...
JOINT: Let me guess. You don't know what you want, right? Nothing ever changes.
ALEXANDRA: No. I know exactly what I want.
JOINT: Then sit right down and we'll...
ALEXANDRA: But I haven't been exactly honest with you.
JOINT: I don't want your honesty, I want your flesh. Have a seat here while I go warm up the gun.
ALEXANDRA: Joint, I know who you are. I know everything about you. I've even seen your work.
JOINT: You've seen my work?
ALEXANDRA: And I know what makes you so special. You know, it's not every day you come across a tattoo artist who is totally blind. (*Joint lets his blindness show for the first time: He knocks into a chair and feels his way to the window. Long Pause.*) You were a bit of an underground celebrity back in the city. (*Joint laughs cynically.*) Joint Abaris: the blind tattoo artist. (*Pause.*)
JOINT: Are you from the media?
ALEXANDRA: No, I'm here because I admire you. And because I have a problem and I think you're the only one who can help me.
JOINT: With what?
ALEXANDRA: With this... (*Alexandra throws opens her coat. Long pause.*)
JOINT: Yeah. Hey, I'm blind, remember?
ALEXANDRA: Mr. Abaris, this is not my body.

SCENE 4

Bus stop.

WIDOW: Well?
COP: Well, what?
WIDOW: What is it?
COP: What is what?
WIDOW: What is it that you're looking for?
COP: What makes you think...
WIDOW: You don't wait at the bus stop unless you are looking for a ride on the bus and we've already established that a ride on the bus is not what you are looking for. And you've got to be looking for something, so I wonder what it may be?
COP: I'm not looking for anything.
WIDOW: You're not from around here...
COP: No. No, I'm not...
WIDOW: And you're not looking for a ride on the bus. *(They both stare in opposite directions. Long pause.)* Is she beautiful?
COP: Who?
WIDOW: I bet she's a real looker! Am I right? Am I? *(Cop looks away.)* I was beautiful once.
COP: I'm sure you were.
WIDOW: Oh yes. I was. *(Cop shrugs. Widow turns to Cop.)* Do you think I was as beautiful then as she is now? *(Cop turns away. Fade.)*

SCENE 5

JOINT: Are you as crazy as you sound, lady?
ALEXANDRA: No, you don't understand. Somebody screwed up. I was born into this body by accident.
JOINT: Oh good. That makes it better.
ALEXANDRA: It doesn't fit me. It's too elegant. And graceful. It would be fine for someone else, but it doesn't fit me. *(Pause.)* There's this girl. I know... well, I don't really know her, she just works in a bakery in my neighbourhood. She's a quiet girl. She works every single day, and it's the most amazing thing. Nobody notices her. Nobody notices as she moves from the cash to the kitchen. And nobody notices when she goes from the kitchen to the window. But every week, she has a brand new hairstyle. Or she's dyed it, or tied it up with flowers, I mean, she tries. But it doesn't matter, because when she dumps pans of bagels into the bin, they only notice the bagels. *(Pause.)* That girl has my body. *(Pause.)*
JOINT: So do you still want a tattoo or...?
ALEXANDRA: Joint, I need your help.
JOINT: Help you how?
ALEXANDRA: I want you to make me invisible. *(Pause.)*
JOINT: What?
ALEXANDRA: I want you to make me invisible.
   (Fade out.)

SCENE 6

Cop is turned away. Widow is turned away. Cop turns to widow.

COP: Have you seen her?
WIDOW: What makes you think that I've seen her?
COP: I'm only asking. It's a pretty small town. I'd imagine a stranger would be kind of obvious in such a small place.
WIDOW: I haven't seen her.
COP: Then I'd better get looking. *(Cop moves to get up.)*
WIDOW: She's not in any trouble, is she? *(Cop stops. Turns.)*
COP: No, not really. She's just lost. And I'm going to bring her home. *(Cop looks away. Widow turns to him.)*
WIDOW: You're here to rescue her?
COP: Yeah, sure. Whatever. Have you seen her?
WIDOW: Are you a prince?
COP: What?
WIDOW: You know, a prince! The son of a king. Are you a Prince?
COP: Yeah, sure, sure. I'm a prince. Have you seen my friend?
WIDOW: Oh, I just knew it! A prince! How exciting. Is that what the "p" stands for?
COP: The "p"?
WIDOW: On your ring. "P," for prince, right?
COP: Uh, no.
WIDOW: What does it stand for?
COP: Peter.
WIDOW: Peter. That's your name, is it?

COP: No.
WIDOW: Prince Peter?
COP: No.
WIDOW: Who's Peter then? (*Pause.*)
COP: Ma'am... please. I just want to...
WIDOW: Where's your horse? (*Cop turns to her.*)
WIDOW: If you're a real prince, you must have a horse. You know, a valiant steed. All princes ride valiant steeds. Everybody knows that. Where's yours? (*Pause.*)
COP: I don't really want anyone to know that I'm a prince, so I left my steed back at the castle. I'm trying to lie low. Now, if you've seen my friend, please tell me about it. If you haven't then I must be on my way. (*Cop and widow stare at one another. Pause.*)
WIDOW: Have you ever been turned into a frog?
COP: Okay, I gotta go... (*Cop gets up.*)
WIDOW: Now that I think about it, there is one young woman staying with me. (*Widow looks away. Cop turns to her.*) I run the local Bed and Breakfast. It's right over there. Just down the road. (*Pause.*) Oh my. I hope you don't need a room. I'm afraid I'm full tonight. All booked up. No vacancy tonight, I'm afraid.
COP: I don't need a room.
WIDOW: I'm the only place in town.
COP: This girl. A tall girl?
WIDOW: Why, yes. Tall. Tall and graceful. Like a ballerina. And I'll have you know a little secret. (*Widow beckons with her finger. Cop moves in close.*) I could have been a ballerina. (*She stands.*) Yes, sir! I was born with the music in me. (Begins dancing.) Blessed with the gift of rhythm. I would have been a big star too. A beloved ballerina! What a dream! (*Widow stares straight ahead.*) But you can't put your kid through college with money you earn in your dreams... (*She sits back down.*) I own the bed and breakfast now.
COP: And my friend? She's there, now?
WIDOW: The ballerina?

COP: Yeah. The ballerina.
WIDOW: Oh, no. She went out around nine.
COP: But she'll be back tonight?
WIDOW: Yes. But you mustn't call for her tonight. It's too late. There are no visitors after nine. That's the rule. And don't think that just because you're a prince you deserve any special favours. *(Widow turns away.* That blue-blooded mumbo jumbo won't work with me. *(Pause.)* I don't care who you think you are, bloody pretentious jet set, there are no visitors after nine! *(Widow turns to cop. Cop turns to widow.)* Nothing personal, of course. It's just a policy…
COP: Fine. I'll call for her in the morning then.
WIDOW: In the morning?
COP: Yes. In the morning.
WIDOW: That will be fine. *(Widow look away. Cop stands.)* Anytime after nine will be fine.
COP: Did she say where she was going? *(She turns to him.)*
WIDOW: Tonight, you mean? *(He turns to her. Fade.)*

SCENE 7

A talk show set. Two chairs, table, coffee mugs. There is a video monitor to the left of the interviewing area, playing a live feed of the show. A fully functional applause sign. House lights come up and floor director runs down through the audience from the back of the house.

FLOOR DIRECTOR: Alright, ladies and gentlemen, we are on the air in fifteen seconds. Let's not be shy. And remember when the applause sign lights up, we need to hear you. Cameras rolling. And we're ready... in five, four, three... *(Applause sign flashes. Host is seated at desk. Beside him sits sidekick.)*

HOST: Ladies and gentleman, we've got a very special show for you tonight. In an attempt to inject some culture into the mindless crap that we bring into your homes every week, we've got a visual artist on our show. *(Audience boos.)* Wait, wait, wait. I wouldn't bore you with that crap, would I? Trust me, this is no ordinary visual artist. First of all, his art is — are you ready for this? — tattoo... *(Audience titters.)* And secondly — and this is the kicker — he's blind. *(Audience cheers.)* Ladies and gentleman, a warm welcome for this crazy cat, Mr. Joint Abaris. *(Applause sign flashes. Sidekick runs across stage to Joint and pins a microphone to his shirt, as he is seated.)* Mr. Abaris, welcome to the show!

JOINT: Call me Joint.

HOST: So, Joint, I gotta ask. How does a blind man... at what point in a blind man's life does he stop and say...

"I'm blind... Maybe I should be a tattoo artist!" *(Audience titters.)*

JOINT: There's really not a lot of literature on how to become a tattoo artist. It just sort of came to me, and I've been doing it ever since.

HOST: Okay, good. But, you're blind!

JOINT: I understood from a very early age, the human urge for individuality.

HOST: Wow.

JOINT: You see, a paradox exists inside of us. We so badly want to be unique, but we're so afraid to be different. And the typical tattoo artist has only made this paradox worse.

HOST: How so?

JOINT: By forgetting the purpose of our work. The use of templates, for instance. A tattoo loses all of its purpose once it has been applied to more than one person. It's an artist's job to constantly challenge and redefine what is beautiful. Not to countlessly reproduce tired images.

HOST: So as a blind tattoo artist, what's your specialty? The straight line? *(Laughter.)* "I call this one the skinny snake." *(Laughter and applause.)*

JOINT: I have no specialty. I wonder if you're listening. I never create the same tattoo twice.

HOST: Wait, wait, wait... you're telling me you've never done the same tattoo twice?

JOINT: That's what I said. Would you like me to tattoo it on you?

HOST: Wait, wait, wait... lemme get this straight. Let's say two big, beefy bikers come into your shop, okay? And they tell you that they want the same tattoo... like, they both want two skinny snakes, okay... you mean to tell me that you're going to tell them they can't have it? What'dya weigh, a hundred pounds? I mean, no offence but you're a bit of a skinny snake yourself. *(Laughter.)*

JOINT: First of all, your example of bikers wanting a tattoo is cliché. Tattooing is not a decoration for outlaws. It's much more important than that. Tattooing is the process of defining our individualism. The art of tattooing is the finishing touch in the creation of the body.

HOST: The creation of the body? Are you comparing tattoo artists to God?

JOINT: Polynesian mythology tells us that humans learned tattooing from the gods. We're not gods... but we are craftsmen commissioned by God.

HOST: Craftsman commissioned by God? This guy is unbelievable. Tell me, if God has a tattoo, where is it? (*Laughter. To Joint.*) Is it on his ass? *(To audience.)* I bet it's on his ass. (*Laughter and applause.*)

JOINT: Different cultures have different beliefs. Personally, I tattoo in search of perfect beauty. The ideal. But historically, the primary function of tattooing was camouflage. Protection.

HOST: I feel like I need to be protected from you... SECURITY! *(Laughter.)*

JOINT: All I'm saying is that tattooing is God-like in that the tattoo artist beholds God's work and then modifies it.

HOST: Okay, drawing an anchor on Popeye's forearm isn't my idea of divinity, but what do I know...? I don't work for God. I didn't even know he was hiring! *(Laughter.)*

JOINT: One does not draw with a tattooing needle.

HOST: And that's another thing. Why would anyone, who's not completely snapped, want to be poked continuously by a needle?

JOINT: It's good to have a wound in life. It reminds us of our impermanence.

HOST: And that reminds me... I've gotta call my therapist.

JOINT: This is the mediocrity that I'm talkin' about— right here.

HOST: I'm mediocre? This is my show! I run the whole thing! How am I mediocre?

JOINT: By making concessions according to the dictates of public opinion. *(Joint rises from his seat.)* You like to think that by being so outspoken that you're the leader, but you are not the author of this story, sir. You are merely a scribe.

TATTOO JOINT

HOST: I'm a what? What did he call me?
(Joint stumbles off the set. Sidekick follows him. Audience howls. Floor director crosses set waving his arms.)

FLOOR DIRECTOR: Set for commercial... *(Whispering)* ...set for commercial.

HOST: Whoa! Well... *(Pause. Applause sign and music – opening bars of "Born to Be Wild" by Steppenwolf.)* What a temper on the little fella! Weird little guy! Ladies and gentlemen, a big round of applause for God's tattoo artist – whatever his name was... *(Music stops.)*

FLOOR DIRECTOR: OKAY, we're clear. *(As lights fade.)*

HOST: What did that guy call me? Hey, can I get a Pellegrino? CAN SOMEBODY GET ME A PELLEGRINO? *(Fade out.)*

SCENE 8

Alexandra stands upstage beside grooming table, under a white spotlight.

ALEXANDRA: Where...? Here...? *(Flash goes.)*
PHOTOGRAPHER *(Voice over)*: Cross your arms, darling.
ALEXANDRA: Like this?
PHOTOGRAPHER *(Voice over):* No... behind your back. That's it. *(Flash goes.)*
ALEXANDRA: Stick out my...? *(She sticks out her chest. Flash goes.)*
PHOTOGRAPHER *(Voice over)*: That's right. Now hold your head up...
ALEXANDRA: Like this? *(Flash goes.)* Lift my skirt? *(Flash goes.)* Higher? *(Flash goes.)* Show my butt and my boobs? At the same time? *(Flash goes.)* Bend those knees. *(Flash goes.)* Suck that belly in. *(Flash goes.)* Show some teeth. *(Flash goes.)* And try to look natural.

SCENE 9

Joint's Tattoo Joint.

ALEXANDRA: I want you to make me invisible— because I hate the attention that this body attracts. I can't even go out for a cup of coffee without causing some kind of commotion. And people treat me like I'm a photograph in a magazine. I don't want that kind of attention. I want to walk the streets unnoticed. Invisible Joint. Like the girl in the bakery.
JOINT: I'm a tattoo artist. I don't make people invisible.
ALEXANDRA: "The tattoo artist beholds God's handiwork and then alters it, in any way he sees fit."
JOINT: That's just pompous. Who said that?
ALEXANDRA: You did. Joint, I know what you're capable of. I've seen your work.
JOINT: You've seen my work? It's pretty hard to come by.
ALEXANDRA: A few years ago, back in the city, you worked at a tattoo parlour on George Street.
JOINT: Chuck's.
ALEXANDRA: Yeah. Chuck's Tattoo.
JOINT: Did you know that I had to hide the fact that I was blind to work in that toilet! Can you imagine? Having to keep secret your greatest asset, and all of your God-given talent, to keep a job working for somebody else!
ALEXANDRA: Joint, while you were there, you did some work for a friend of mine.
JOINT: She got upset with me, right?
ALEXANDRA: You remember her?

JOINT: No. When I worked at Chuck's, they all became upset with me.

ALEXANDRA: She asked you for a butterfly and…

JOINT: A butterfly! So cliché. All the girls want butterflies. Because butterflies are dainty. A symbol of femininity. An emblem of freedom and metamorphosis. People don't want the kind of tattoos I create. Because my tattoos are different. But the main reason people get tattoos in the first place is to be different. Butterflies! All of the girls want butterflies, and do you know what the guys want? Panthers! Panthers! Sleek, graceful, powerful, mysterious, virile, big. Game. Hunters. Fat and smelly animals, that's what I say. *(Pause.)* Tell me more about your friend. *(Fade out.)*

SCENE 10

Fade in stage right to reveal Chuck's Tattoo. Patron 1 is alone, looking around. Joint enters.

JOINT: May I help you?
PATRON 1: I'm looking for Chuck... (Long pause. Joint "stares" blankly.) Are you Chuck?
JOINT: I'm Joint.
PATRON 1: Oh. *(Patron 1 looks around.)* I hope I'm in the right place. There are so many tattoo parlours downtown, and they all look the same to me. (Pause.) Joint "stares" blankly. Somebody recommended Chuck...
JOINT: Chuck is the owner. But he's out today.
PATRON 1: Oh. Well, I was thinking about getting one...
JOINT: A tattoo?
PATRON 1: Yeah.
Joint pulls his tattoo gun from a holster worn around his waist and points to the curtain.
JOINT: Come back here. We'll get started.
PATRON 1: Well... I'm not quite sure what I want yet.
JOINT: You're not sure what you want. *(Joint puts gun back into sheath.)*
PATRON 1: Not just yet.
JOINT: But you're here.
PATRON 1: Yeah.
JOINT: And yet, you don't know what you want?
PATRON 1: Not just yet.
JOINT: But you're here.
PATRON 1: It's a big decision, right? I mean...

JOINT: Whether or not to go to a tattoo parlour is a big decision?
PATRON 1: No, going isn't such a big deal but...
JOINT: And why do you go to a tattoo parlour?
PATRON 1: To get a tattoo, I guess...
JOINT: And here you are... *(Pause. Patron1 considers.)*
PATRON 1: How about a butterfly!
JOINT: A butterfly?
PATRON 1: Yeah, that's why I'm here. To get a butterfly. It's kinda like a symbol for me, you know?
JOINT: Sit down here a minute.

(She sits facing audience. Joint circles around her until he is behind her and facing the audience.)

PATRON 1: I just left my boyfriend, you know. He was always trying to control me. Everything I did was like a hassle, you know? Like this one time, I went out to sing Karaoke with a girlfriend, right, I mean, I just wanted to sing Karaoke, ya know? *(Joint stands behind her and puts his hands on her face. Stage darkens except for soft spotlight on chair.)*
PATRON 1: What are you doing?
JOINT: I'm seeing you. I need to get a sense of you, before we begin.
PATRON 1: Oh... 'kay... Anyway, he just didn't trust me. That was his problem. He always thought I was going to cheat on him. *(Pause.)* I mean, I did cheat on him, that's the funny part. Two times. But he never found out about it! But still, he didn't trust me. And he made everything a hassle. If I wanted to go somewhere— anywhere— it was a hassle. If I wanted to try something new, anything, it was a hassle. Like last summer. I was going to take this art course, ya know?
JOINT: An art course?
PATRON 1: Yeah. I'm a painter. Well. I paint. I've always liked to paint. I mean, I've never shown my stuff, ya know, like in a museum, but I have a few hanging around in my room. And all of my roommates tell me they're awesome.

I just thought I'd like to take a course, you know, to learn stuff. You know?

JOINT: Like how to paint butterflies?

PATRON 1: Sure. Maybe. Anyway, my boyfriend made such a big deal about it. He said the course was too expensive, he said the supplies cost too much. He said no girlfriend of his was going to sit around drawing naked people all day. He was always putting down artists. He says that artists are society's rejects. Lazy misfits.

JOINT: Does he have a tattoo?

PATRON 1: Yeah. A panther. It's real artsy too. No matter where you are in the room, it looks like it's looking at you…

JOINT: …I'm ready.

PATRON 1: Okay. Should I…

JOINT: Just come back here and we'll get started.

PATRON 1 *(Still seated)*: Shouldn't I tell you what kind of butterfly I want?

JOINT: I don't see why.

(They move behind curtain. Stage darkens. Bright light behind them projects their silhouette onto curtain. Silence. Sound of needle buzzing.)

PATRON 1: Hey, stop! STOP!

(Idling needle buzzes.)

JOINT: Yes?

PATRON 1: You're not even looking at me!

JOINT: Would it make you feel better if I were looking at you?

PATRON 1: Yes! Yes, it would make me feel better! Of course it would make me feel better! *(Lights flash erratically, as needle drones. Fade.)*

SCENE 11

ALEXANDRA: He kept her behind that curtain for seven hours. For seven hours. He slaved over her. All she wanted was a butterfly. But it was beautiful. Like nothing you've ever seen. At first glance, it was just colours. But as she moved – when the light caught it – it became a picture. A woman crawling away from an old stone tower. She was dressed in a long beaded gown, like a princess – but crawling on the ground. And covered in mud. *(Pause.)* When I looked at that tattoo, I saw the real person on the inside… That's what I want him to do for me. Find the real person inside and bring it out. *(Fade out.)*

SCENE 12

Stage left snaps in to reveal library. Peter far right of stage holding a stack of four books. Alexandra enters from darkness.

ALEXANDRA: Can I help you with something? *(Peter stops and stares at her. Drops his books. Alexandra approaches to help him.)*
PETER *(Back to his senses):* Sorry.
ALEXANDRA: Never mind.
PETER: I'm... Peter.
ALEXANDRA: Peter.
PETER: Peter Beset.
ALEXANDRA: I'm Alex. Alexandria. *(Peter stares. Alexandra moves to checkout counter. Begins the check-out procedure.)*
PETER: So... uh... do you like being a librarian?
ALEXANDRA: I like it well enough.
PETER: Must get a little lonely.
ALEXANDRA: Lonely?
PETER: It's so quiet. Nobody. Nothing but books.
ALEXANDRA: I don't mind quiet.
PETER: It's so big and empty in here. It's like being locked away in the tower of a spooky old castle. So solitary. *(Pause.)*
ALEXANDRA: I don't mind solitary.
PETER: If you want. I could... would you like to get a coffee sometime?
ALEXANDRA: I don't think so.

PETER: Sorry. It's just that you're so... Look at me, I can't even speak. I'm overwhelmed. You're so beautiful.
ALEXANDRA: I don't think so.
PETER: No, I mean it. You're a knock-out!
ALEXANDRA: No. I mean, I don't think we can meet.
PETER *(Instinctly)*: Oh.
ALEXANDRA: The library keeps me so busy. It's all of these books. Besides, isn't that a wedding ring on your finger?
PETER: This? Yes. Why, yes. We're having difficulties. Please, just meet me for coffee. You like coffee, don't you?
ALEXANDRA: I like French Roast.
PETER: Great! French Roast it is then...
ALEXANDRA: But I'm not going to have French Roast with you.
PETER: But...
ALEXANDRA: You're married.
PETER *(Comically)*: Yes, but the problems...
ALEXANDRA: I think you should take your books and go home to your wife. *(Peter picks up the books and stares at Alexandra, before exiting. Alexandra moves off stage. Fade.)*

SCENE 13

From darkness:

SPEAKING CLOCK: THE TIME IS ELEVEN-THIRTY P.M. ELEVEN-THIRTY IS THE TIME. *(Fade in to Joint's Tattoo Joint. Joint takes a seat in front of grooming table. Begins brushing his hair. Alexandra approaches.)*
ALEXANDRA: What are you doing?
JOINT: I'm brushing my hair.
ALEXANDRA: Yes, but...
JOINT: I'm getting ready for bed. It's eleven-thirty and I have to open the shop in the morning at nine. And Apollo is exhausted. Look at him.
ALEXANDRA: You're looking in the mirror.
JOINT: And...
ALEXANDRA: Well you're blind, for starters.
JOINT *(Proudly)*: As a bat! *(Joint goes to shelf and grabs another can of tomatoes.)*
ALEXANDRA: Then why the mirror?
JOINT: Almost literally, blind as a bat. But bats can see. They just see differently. Bats have made blindness their advantage.
ALEXANDRA: And blindness is your advantage?
JOINT *(Fiddling with can opener)*: Yes. Art is spoiled as soon as it is seen by other people. It's no longer pure. Because no matter how open-minded one is, one can't help but pass some sort of judgement. And that cheapens it. *(Joint drops can opener and feels around for it.)*

JOINT: Ideal beauty can be seen only with the mind's eye. *(Joint tries to continue but falls to the floor in convulsions. Once the fit subsides, Joint breathing heavily, eats a tomato and tries to stand.)* Get out. Just go. *(Alexandra stands motionless. Disoriented, Joint yells in the wrong direction.)* And now I suppose you're deaf? Is that it? I asked you to leave. *(Alexandra stands motionless. Joint gets to his feet and reorientates. Regains composure.)* Don't bother trying to befuddle me. *(Sarcastic.)* The pleasing bouquet of your perfume betrays your attempts to manipulate me.

ALEXANDRA: I'm not trying to manipulate you.

JOINT: Then do me a favour and disappear just as candidly as you arrived. *(Pause.)*

ALEXANDRA: Joint.

JOINT: Just go. *(Joint, suffering from a small aftershock of his attack, stumbles and falls to the ground. Alexandra rushes to him.)*

ALEXANDRA: Joint. *(He pushes her away and gets up on his own. Pause.)*

JOINT: I have seizures. Okay? What's the big deal? Have you never seen a blind tattoo artist with epilepsy? *(Pause. Alexandra holds him. He concedes.)*

ALEXANDRA: A seizure caused your blindness. *(Pause. Joint pulls away from her.)*

JOINT: I don't know. I was probably two… or three… and a prolonged fit left me in the dark. I wound up on the doorstep of an orphanage. I don't know how! Left in the care of people who had no time to tend to a convulsing simpleton. They just left me there. Alone. In the darkness. *(Stage left. Orphanage mother and doctor enter, veiled by shadows.)*

ORPHANAGE MOTHER: He just sits there, all day long. *(Rocking back and forth on the floor.)*

DOCTOR: He won't tell you what's wrong?

ORPHANAGE MOTHER: He doesn't even speak, doctor. Put food or a toy in front of him and he just ignores them.

DOCTOR: How does he behave with the other children?

ORPHANAGE MOTHER: They're afraid of him. Because he's so strange. He doesn't even try!

DOCTOR: Does he often do that to his eyes?

ORPHANAGE MOTHER: Yes. He's always doing that. He pokes his fingers right into his eyes until they get infected. Why does he do that? He won't stop doing that.

DOCTOR: He can't see.

ORPHANAGE MOTHER: What?

DOCTOR: He's blind. *(Orphanage mother turns to him.)* A blind child sticks his fingers into his eyes because it causes what he thinks are flashes of light. He's trying to see.

SCENE 14

Joint's Tattoo Joint.

JOINT *(Rubbing his eyes.)* The flashes of light became colours and the colours form into shapes. The shapes become...
ALEXANDRA: ...Images and the images become your art. *(Alexandra goes to him. He is reluctant but concedes. She holds him.)*
JOINT: I might be able to help you, but I need some time. Do you have somewhere to stay tonight?
ALEXANDRA: I have a room. *(She points absently.)*
JOINT: Come back tomorrow after we open. I'll have an answer for you then.
SPEAKING CLOCK: THE TIME IS MIDNIGHT. MIDNIGHT IS THE TIME. *(Alexandra doesn't move.)*
JOINT: We open at nine. *(Alexandra nods and exits slowly. Joint relocks the door. He moves the chairs back to their original positions and sits back at the table and picks up a brush. Begins brushing his hair. A knock at the door.)* Busy fuckin' day. We're closed... *(More knocking.)* We close at nine. *(More knocking.)* Is it past nine p.m.? Yes, it is. WE'RE CLOSED. *(Cop appears behind Joint.)* You're not here for a tattoo, are you?
COP: A tattoo?
JOINT: Yes.
COP: No. This is a...
JOINT: ...a tattoo parlour, yes.
COP: You should have a sign.
JOINT: I had one.

TATTOO JOINT

COP: What happened to it?

JOINT: It's gone.

COP: Gone?

JOINT: Vanished.

COP: Disappeared?

JOINT: Gone.

COP: That's odd. *(Pause.)*

JOINT: Is that all then? I've got to get ready for bed. We open at nine.

COP: Actually, no. I'm looking for somebody. A girl.

JOINT: A girl?

COP: Yes. I wonder if you've seen her?

JOINT: If I've seen her?

COP: Have you? *(Joint "stares" at Cop.)* It's very important that I find her. I have this photograph. *(Walks behind Joint holding photograph.)* Does she look familiar?

JOINT *(Not looking at picture):* Not really, no...

COP: Sir?

JOINT: Yes?

COP: You didn't even look at the photograph.

JOINT *(Turns and pretends to really study picture):* I can say quite honestly, I have not seen her.

COP: Seems a little odd.

JOINT: What?

COP: Well, earlier, I was talking to an old lady who did see her. Rented her a room, as a matter of fact. She said she may have come this way.

JOINT: This way?

COP: That's what she said.

JOINT: Looking for a tattoo?

COP: I can't say for sure.

JOINT: It sure would have been nice if she did come this way. Business hasn't been exactly booming, lately.

COP: Oh?

JOINT: Haven't had a customer in two years.

COP: Two years?

JOINT: It's just a lull.

COP: But you weren't even gonna let me in.

JOINT: Because we're closed.

COP: But what if I was a customer?

JOINT: So what if you were a customer? We close at nine o'clock. That's just the way things are around...

COP: ...Two fuckin' years? If you haven't had a customer in two fuckin' years, then you'd remember if a lady came in here earlier tonight. *(Cop throws his card on the table.)* Tell you what. Give me a call if you see anything, okay?

JOINT: If I see anything.

COP: Then you call me.

JOINT: Gotcha.

COP: Good. *(Cop and Joint consider one another.)* Two fuckin' years! *(Cop exits. Joint returns to the small table, brushes his hair. Rises. Puts red silk over goldfish bowl, turns out the lights and exits to the bedroom.)*

JOINT: Goodnight, Apollo. See you in the morning.

END OF ACT I

ACT II

SCENE 1

Fade-in to Joint's studio. He is staring out big window. He rises and moves to the door. He waits until:

SPEAKING CLOCK: THE TIME IS NINE A.M. NINE IS THE TIME. *(Joint flips the sign to read OPEN and feeds fish.)*
JOINT: Good morning, Apollo. *(Long pause.)* Did you sleep well? *(Alexandra suddenly appears behind him.)*
ALEXANDRA: Good morning, Mr. Abaris. I'm here. Just like we said. Nine o'clock. Did you get a chance to think? I'm sorry if I seem a little bit brisk this morning. This is a big day for me. I mean, that dependents on you. Am I babbling? I feel as though I'm babbling. I really didn't get much sleep, Mr. Abaris?
JOINT: You're babbling.
ALEXANDRA: What are you doing?
JOINT: I'm working.
ALEXANDRA: Staring out the window is working? Cushy job.
JOINT: It is difficult for a blind man to "stare" at anything.
ALEXANDRA: Then what are you doing?
JOINT: I'm creating a new work. This is how I do it now. *(Pause.)*
ALEXANDRA: Don't you miss actually doing it?
JOINT: I do it every day. I just told you, it's just different, that's all.
ALEXANDRA: I mean real tattoos, on real people. What good is invisible art? Isn't the whole point of it that others can see it? *(Joint gets up and grabs for a can of tomatoes.)*
JOINT: No! It's become that, yes. But that doesn't mean it's right.

SCENE 2

Widow sits alone on bench at bus stop. Enter cop stage left. He sits. He is looking away. She is looking at him.

WIDOW: Any luck?
COP: Any luck?
WIDOW: Yes. Any?
COP: Luck?
WIDOW: Yes.
COP: No. Maybe some.
WIDOW: Some luck?
COP: Maybe. Did you know it's a tattoo parlour?
WIDOW: What is?
COP: That little shop.
WIDOW: What little shop?
COP: Right over there.
WIDOW: Which one?
COP: There's only one.
WIDOW: No. There are two.
COP: But one is a barbershop.
WIDOW: The barbershop is a tattoo parlour?
COP: No, the other one. *(Pause.)*
WIDOW: The one beside the big open space?
COP: Yeah.
WIDOW: I don't think so.
COP: Well, it is.

SCENE 3

Chuck's Tattoo. From darkness:

CHUCK *(Shouting)*: Joint! Joint! Can you come in here please! *(Stage lights rise to reveal Chuck's TATTOO. Patron 2 is pacing, upset. Patron 3 sits in the corner behind a magazine. Joint enters.)*

PATRON 2: That's the fucking guy!

CHUCK: Joint, there seems to have been a bit of a mix-up.

PATRON 2: A mix-up? Mix-up? There is no mix-up, huh? That fucking guy right there, Il n'est pas correct! I should have known he was a phony baloney. He doesn't even have a tattoo. That guy.

CHUCK: Listen. Calm down. We can fix this. We can fix all of this...

PATRON 2: A tattoo artist who has no tattoo? Où est-ce qu'il est ton tatouage, huh? Où est ton tatouage?

CHUCK: Sir, we can fix it, okay. No charge. We'll fix it.

PATRON 2: Listen, okay. I come in here, I say, bien, I want one tattoo behind me and he says okay doke. I take you behind da curtain. I say, bien non! I should speak to you a bit before, huh? He says, me I don't see why. Viens ici behind la curtain, tabernac! I'm pissed.

CHUCK: Dude, this guy says he wanted a tattoo of this image. Bro, it's my Cubic Cross. Our simplest design. The template is right here, man. A simple design.

PATRON 2: Simple design? Simple design! I was on that table for eight fucking hours, huh! Eight fucking hours. That`s not too simple for me, huh?

CHUCK: Sir... I'm going to work this out...

PATRON 2: Crosseur, maybe I should work something on his... fucking... I'm pissed!

CHUCK: Dude, he asked for my Cubic Cross. The Cubic Cross only requires black ink.

PATRON 2: Black ink? Mon sacrement d'ostie chalise de plote salle!

CHUCK: The design you did, on his back has colours, Joint. Colours I've never even seen before. *(Pulling Joint aside and whispering.)* Dude, I don't know how you did that, man, but I want you to take him back there and fix it. My reputation is on the line here. You've got to go back there and fix it, somehow. Okay?

JOINT: It's done.

CHUCK: What?

JOINT: You couldn't possibly add or remove one more drop of ink to it. It's perfect.

CHUCK: Dude, it's not what he wanted. He wanted a black cross. You gave him jumbled colours. It looks like a goddamn taco salad.

PATRON 2: Maybe here come the fucking cops, on you man... bonjour la police... sacrement!

CHUCK: He selected my design, Joint. All you had to do was copy it. That's what we do here. Designs. We let the customer choose and then we apply it. We do not choose designs for them.

JOINT: I didn't choose anything. Look at it. It's not for him. It is him.

CHUCK *(Crescendo):* Joint, this is serious. I gave you a job. I gave you my friendship. I let you live in my storeroom, for chrissake! And this is how you repay me? By constantly pissing off my clients? I musta been outta my fucking mind!

PATRON 2: I'll tell you who's out of his fucking mind... Mon homme-ici le, fucking, rat, cocombre!

CHUCK: I hired you to help me. To take off some of the pressure. And since then I've had nothing but complaints.

JOINT: Chuck, every situation has an irony.

PATRON 2: Mon fucking shit, merde, taber-fuck! I should put your ass at the end of my foot!

CHUCK: That is not art, Joint. Look at that mess. A blind man could design a better tattoo.

PATRON 2: Awwwwww shit!

CHUCK: This is the design he wants. *(Holding the template in front of Joint's face. Pause.)*

JOINT: I can't see it.

CHUCK: You're not even looking!

JOINT: Because I CAN'T SEE IT… just as you can't see my design. We're all blind!

CHUCK: Get out… *(Pause. Chuck grabs Joint and forcefully takes him outside.)*

PATRON 2: I knew I shoulda got my tattoo in Quebec! Ontario gots no culture. *(Patron 2 facing the audience throws off his open over-shirt to reveal his tattooed shoulder to Patron 3 who is sitting behind him. As the lights fade, Patron 3 stands and moves to get a closer look, obviously struck by what she sees.)*

SCENE 4

A female figure is sitting at grooming table, veiled in shadow.

ALEXANDRA: "Pretty takes pains…" That's what my mother used to say. "Pretty takes pains." Every morning she spent hours in front of a mirror, just like this one, fixing herself. Making everything. Pretty. Plucking and squeezing, applying and removing, dying, bleaching, curling, straightening. Transforming. My goodness she was beautiful. *(Pause. Flash goes. Figure rises from table, puts on coat/hat.)* And then, one morning, she hid her hair under a hat, and hid her face behind sunglasses. I asked her where she was going in such a hurry. *(Flash goes.)* She just kissed me on the forehead and gave me an envelope. *(Flash goes. Male figure appears in doorway.)* A strange man was standing by the door. *(Flash goes.)* And they left. *(Flash goes. Male and female figure appear as silhouettes in a passionate embrace behind scrim.)* She didn't even say goodbye. She didn't even look back. She just closed the door and left. I was eight years old. When my father came home I gave him the envelope. He said she was going to spend the summer in Paris and that she would come back in the fall.
JOINT: And did she?
ALEXANDRA: No. But Paris is so beautiful. Especially in the fall.
NURSE *(Voice over):* The doctor will see you now, Miss. *(Alexandra moves to where surgeon is seated at desk, and looking in a file. Surgeon is dressed in full clown garb.)*

TATTOO JOINT

SURGEON: So I see that you're considering surgery. It's nothing to be ashamed about. We all have things about our bodies that we're unhappy with and would like to change. Even me. Look at the size of my feet! *(Pause. Looking in file.)* Now, I'm not quite sure what you want.

ALEXANDRA: Doctor, my body doesn't fit me. *(Pause.)*

SURGEON: You want bigger boobs, right?

ALEXANDRA: No, I certainly do not want bigger boobs.

SURGEON: Liposuction?

ALEXANDRA: No, no.

SURGEON: We could suck some white cheddar right out of the ol' cheese fridge. (He slaps her backside) And you'll be as pretty as a daisy.

ALEXANDRA: I don't want liposuction!

DOCTOR: Hmm. Let's have a look at the request form. Now, you have four choices. *(Surgeon pulls out a large oversized chart upon which is written: CHECK ONE: BOOB JOB, NOSE JOB, TUMMY TUCK, BUTT LIFT.)*

ALEXANDRA: I don't want any of those. Please listen to me. This is not my face. And this is not my body. I was born into this body by accident. It doesn't fit me. What I want from you is… I want you to make me invisible. *(Pause.)*

SURGEON: Invisible huh? What I'm going to do is recommend another kind of doctor. *(Surgeon scribbles on a note pad.)*

ALEXANDRA: Oh God! I don't need a psychiatrist! I'm not crazy, I just want a different face.

SURGEON: A different face! Why didn't you say so? *(Doctor pulls a series of large photographs out from behind desk. He flips to a different one with each new suggestion.)* J. Lo is very popular right now.

ALEXANDRA: No.

SURGEON: Yeah, you're probably right. I make you look like this and you'll be obsolete by the spring. How about something with a little more staying power? *(Picture of Madonna.)*

ALEXANDRA: Oh no.

SURGEON: Okay, too slutty? How about the original? *(Picture of Marilyn Monroe.)*
ALEXANDRA: Hmm... No!
SURGEON: Cher's good?
ALEXANDRA: No.
SURGEON: Spice Girl?
ALEXANDRA: No.
SURGEON: Michael Jackson?
ALEXANDRA: No. *(Picture of coffee mug.)*
SURGEON: Coffee?
ALEXANDRA: What? *(Picture of wine glass.)*
SURGEON: How about dinner?
ALEXANDRA: No! *(Picture of heart.)*
SURGEON: I think I love you! *(Fade.)*

SCENE 5

Bus stop.

WIDOW: A tattoo parlour? In my town? *(Cop nods. Pause.)* There's no sign.
COP: Yes.
WIDOW: No. Look.
COP: I mean, yes, there is no sign.
WIDOW: There should be a sign.
COP: You're probably right. *(Pause.)*
WIDOW: A good business needs a sign. *(Cop shrugs.)* Who does he think he is? Running a business with no sign? *(Cop shrugs.)* The barbershop has a sign. My Bed and Breakfast has a sign. *(Pause.)* I drew it myself. *(Cop nods.)* Imagine. Running a business with no sign. *(Cop shrugs.)* It's just pompous. *(Cop nods.)* Must think an awful lot of himself. *(Cop nods.)* Renegade. *(Longer pause.)* Did she get one?
COP: One what?
WIDOW: The ballerina.
COP: What about her?
WIDOW: Did she get one?
COP: A tattoo?
WIDOW: Yes.
COP: No. She wouldn't get a tattoo. Why would she want a tattoo?
WIDOW: Why would she go to a tattoo parlour if she didn't want a tattoo?
COP: She's not the type.

WIDOW: I can't think of any other reason to go to a tattoo parlour. You don't go to a tattoo parlour to buy toilet paper. You don't go to a tattoo parlour to have your fortune told. *(Widow stands.)* Do you like me in this dress?

COP: It's a lovely dress.

WIDOW: This dress used to get a young man's blood pumping a few years back, if you know what I mean. It wasn't that long ago, you know.

COP: It's lovely.

WIDOW *(Puts her leg up on the bench)*: Don't I have nice legs? These are dancer's legs. Don't you think? These legs used to stop a train in its tracks. Do you still think they could? Maybe?

COP: Maybe.

WIDOW: Don't I remind you of her?

COP: Not really.

WIDOW: Maybe a little? *(Cop considers her.)*

COP: No. *(Widow returns to her seat.)*

WIDOW *(Sadly)*: I'm afraid we haven't progressed at all. In my day, we didn't flaunt our wares the way the girls do today. No, Sir, we maintained an air of innocence. Dignity. Oh sure, we were gawked at, whistled at, and treated as fluffy toys for men to have and to hold. But we kept our dignity! Under long skirts and shirts that had sleeves. Oh, we women have undergone many changes for sure: from slave to happy homemaker; from bra-burning sexual-revolutionary to independent career woman. *(Cop turns to her.)* But progress? I don't think so. No, Sir. For to progress means to move forward and women have only revolved around a circle, and who do you think stands dumbfounded in the centre of that circle? The men. The men, who still regard women as cute and fluffy toys. Women need to realize that they don't need to change themselves – but men. They need to change the men. *(Pause.)*

COP: I've got to find her.

WIDOW: It's funny. I heard Te was blind.

COP: Who?
WIDOW: The renegade.
COP: Blind?
WIDOW: As a bat.
COP *(Turning to face shop):* He didn't tell me that.
WIDOW: I wonder if there's anything else he didn't tell you? *(Pause.)* A business with no sign. Renegade.

SCENE 6

Joint is seated in his chair, heating a tomato over the flame of a candle. There is an open can of tomatoes in his lap.

ALEXANDRA: Joint, why do you choose to do things the hard way? You don't have to live like this. You could come back to the city. We could go back together. You can stay with me until you get back on your feet. You could open a shop in a nice place where there are people.
JOINT: It's too late for that now.
ALEXANDRA: Why? Joint, you don't have to live like this.
JOINT: I've already started. I can't give up now. *(Pause.)*
ALEXANDRA: Then why don't you tattoo on yourself?
JOINT: I can't decide what I want.
ALEXANDRA: You can't decide? You? The one who is always hammering others for their indecisiveness?
JOINT: In my search to redefine beauty, I haven't been able to find anything beautiful enough to tattoo onto myself.
ALEXANDRA: So tattoo on me! Why not? I want one. You need the work. Create some of that beauty on me.
JOINT: You don't want me to create beauty. You want me to destroy it. That's not my job.
ALEXANDRA: Who's job is it then?
JOINT: Time! Time is the only eradicator of Beauty!
ALEXANDRA: I can't wait for time. I won't make it. You're asking me to wait until my life is over, before I begin living it. I need to change now.
JOINT: That seems a little extreme.

ALEXANDRA: Extreme? Extreme? WHAT DO YOU KNOW ABOUT EXTREME? You've buried your head in the sand for two years.

JOINT: The mainline of the creative endeavor is done in solitude!

ALEXANDRA: What creative endeavor? Sitting in a chair? Staring out a window?

JOINT: The current state of Beauty is in turmoil and I'm trying to fix it!

ALEXANDRA: No, you're not! You're hiding from it. Ignoring it – everything! What about friends? Or someone to love you?

JOINT: I seek in solitude that which I cannot find in the company of others. Serenity. Sincerity. Clarity.

ALEXANDRA: You're afraid.

JOINT: No.

ALEXANDRA: You avoid the real world.

JOINT: As a safeguard from ignorance!

ALEXANDRA: In here, you're safe. Oh, sure! You're a bloody genius! But as soon as you go through that door, you're not so special.

JOINT: This is a place of retreat, where one can recoup one's poise.

ALEXANDRA: Bullshit! You're afraid! Because you go out there and you're forced to compare yourself to other people and you find out, you're nobody. You're a failure. A misfit. A freak. *(Long pause.)*

JOINT: If only I could be as level-headed as you! The girl who sells me bagels has my body and I have all of these memories of Paris but I've never been to Paris and I'm going to take a vacation in a town who's only attraction is a big, open space! *(Pause.)*

ALEXANDRA: You're a coward. *(Long pause.)*

JOINT: I'm a coward? How do you figure? I live like this as a proclamation of independence! An assertion of will! A defiance against the Tattoo Hanging Committee of the salons – if there was one. I will never go back there. I would rather rot.

ALEXANDRA: That's fine. But don't pretend to know what I go through in the real world. You can't know. Because you've quit on it. *(Pause. Alexandra moves into spotlight and speaks right in Joint's ear.)* And you have no idea the damage I have caused. *(Fade.)*

SCENE 7

Library set. Fade in to find Peter waiting at the desk with two Styrofoam cups. After a moment, Alexandra enters.

PETER: I thought if you didn't want to go out and get coffee with me, I would go out and get coffee and bring it to you!
ALEXANDRA: Peter, I can't accept that.
PETER: It's just coffee! *(Pause.)*
ALEXANDRA: Still, I can't accept it.
PETER: Come on. It's just coffee. There are no diamonds in it.
ALEXANDRA: Alright. As long as you understand that it's just coffee.
PETER: But it's not just coffee. *(Alexandra is about to object.)* It's French Roast! Now I know you like French Roast, so you can't object. But what I don't know is how you like it? I brought lots of everything. *(Pause.)* Sugar? *(Pause.)* Cream? *(Pause.)* Black? *(Pause.)* C'mon.
ALEXANDRA: Two creams. One sugar. Please. *(Pause.)* That's how my mother drank French Roast. One sugar and two creams.
PETER: Two and one it is then. To your mother... *(They touch cups and she sips and Peter moves his hand to her cheek.)* Do you know how long I've been waiting to see this face?
ALEXANDRA: Okay, that's enough.
PETER: Alexandra, c'mon! I can't help myself. I don't even want to. You are the most exquisite thing I have ever seen.
ALEXANDRA: You don't even know me.
PETER: But I do know you!

ALEXANDRA: We've only just met.

PETER: And already, I know you. Quite remarkable if you ask me.

ALEXANDRA: And you're married.

PETER: Wrong again.

ALEXANDRA: Yes. *(Pause.)* Where is your wedding ring?

PETER: I took it off.

ALEXANDRA: Why?

PETER: Because I filed for divorce. Just before I went for coffee. *(He sips.)*

ALEXANDRA: What?

PETER: I filed for divorce.

ALEXANDRA: When?

PETER: Just now. Then I went for coffee.

ALEXANDRA: Did you tell your wife?

PETER: No.

ALEXANDRA: Why not?

PETER: I just told you! Because I went for coffee. *(Pause.)* My lawyer will call my wife. It's all done. He'll arrange everything. *(He sips.)* Custody and everything. *(He sips.)*

ALEXANDRA: Custody?

PETER: Of my daughter.

ALEXANDRA: Peter!

PETER: We can see her on weekends. It'll be perfect. You're going to love her. (Singing.) Coffee's getting cold... *(He sips.)*

ALEXANDRA: This isn't because... You two were having problems right? You said so. This has nothing to do – nothing to do...

PETER: With you? Alexandra, this has everything to do with you.

ALEXANDRA: You were having difficulties, Peter. You said so.

PETER: As soon as I saw that face...

ALEXANDRA: Please don't.

PETER: I knew it was you. *(Peter touches her face with both hands. She pulls away.)*

ALEXANDRA: Peter, stop. *(Long pause.)*

PETER: I love it when you say my name. *(Pause.)* Say it again. *(Pause.)* C'mon. Say it again.
ALEXANDRA: Get out of here.
PETER: What?
ALEXANDRA: Go home to your wife.
PETER: Alex, I don't have a wife. I filed for divorce, remember? Before I went for coffee.
ALEXANDRA: You do have a wife! You do! And a daughter. Go away from me. Go home. Go home to them. *(Alexandra walks to the shadows of stage right leaving Peter alone with the coffee cups. He contemplates, staring out into the audience. Fade.)*

SCENE 8

Fade in stage right. Alexandra facing audience, Joint facing window.

ALEXANDRA: We'd just met. I didn't even go out with him. I didn't even want to. His wife said she'd never let him divorce her.
SPEAKING CLOCK: THE TIME IS TEN-FORTY-FIVE A.M. TEN-FORTY-FIVE IS THE TIME.
ALEXANDRA: He had it all but he couldn't see it. He could only see me. And now it's gone.
JOINT: Gone?
ALEXANDRA: Vanished. *(Pause.)* He killed her. He killed them both. His wife and his innocent little girl.

SCENE 9

Library set. Peter stands alone in spotlight holding a book.

PETER *(To audience):* You can't blame me for this. You don't blame me for this. Do you? This is how I was brought up. This is how we were all brought up. C'mon! We were raised reading fairy tales, man! Are we not the TV generation? What about advertisements? Pop music? Hollywood? Let's face it, our perspective on reality is a little skewed. Matters of the heart come down to: "I'm in the Mood for Love." "Why Do Fools Fall In Love?" "Mad Love," "Addicted to Love," "To Russia with Love," "Love and Basketball," "Everyone Says I Love You," "Jennifer Love Hewitt," *I Love Lucy, The Love Boat, Love's Labour's Lost, Beauty and the fucking Beast. (Pause.)* You want a story? I'll tell you a goddamned story. Once upon a time, in the dead of winter, when flakes of snow were falling, it happened that a king's son was passing by. He rode upon a trusty steed, because all princes ride upon trusty steeds, and he rode with passion and determination because he was on a quest. Long, long ago when our prince was just a boy and still discovering the marvelous things of the world, he had a wonderful dream. He dreamt of a beautiful young princess, dressed in a long beaded gown, and standing beside a large stone tower. The prince called out to the princess, but she did not turn to him. And he chased after her but the more he ran, the farther away she seemed. "Please turn around only that I may see your face" he called to her, but she stood perfectly still staring down into the mud. The princess was so fair and held such a lingering presence that when the boy awoke from his dream, he could think of nothing else. I mean, he was just a boy, sure, but he loved her. Without even seeing her face, he loved her. And so it became his quest. To find her. She was his ideal woman. *(He slams the book shut.)* But so many things get in the way of a dream. Your parents. There's pressure. Your friends. Sometimes, the people you care about the most just serve to remind you of how lonely you are and nobody wants to wind up alone. And before you know it, you're married. You have a wife and a job and bills and more bills and a crying kid always needs something. *(Pause.)* You, gentlemen, are with me on this, right? We all have an ideal woman. And I got a fistful of gold coins that says it sure as hell isn't the one you're sitting beside right now. Is it? *(Pause.)* Aw, c'mon. Don't you look at me like that. Like I'm some poor crackbrained dupe and different from you. We all need a damsel in distress. Maybe I should get back to the story. Time has worked its undermining magic on our young prince. He no longer resides in a castle, he lives in a duplex and everyday he kisses his wife, he hugs his kid, and rides off to work. He sits in a chair. He sharpens pencils. He's traded in his gothic finger gauntlets for Isotoner gloves and his trusty valiant steed for a goddamned Oldsmobile Intrigue, but he had a quest! He had dreams. He was not put on this earth to crunch numbers for some fat bastard who lives half of the year on a beach in the Canary Islands. And there is nothing intriguing about a goddamned Oldsmobile. *(Pause.)* When did our hero get to be so old? And how did all of those dreams get so far behind him? *(Pause.)* I turned forty-five this week. My wife threw me a surprise party. My brother was there. A couple of the neighbours. Some friends of the kid. And my birthday present? Three tickets to France. See, my wife's always wanted to go to Paris. And we were finally going to go. As a family. I mean, that's why I was in that goddamned library to begin with. I was looking for books on travelling through Paris. *(Pause.)* I was looking for books and I found her. She was just standing there, waiting, just as she was in the dream. She's not locked up in any stone tower, she's in a library. And she's not in a long, beaded gown, she's in a sundress, but there is no doubt she's the one. And that face. It's absolutely perfect! "Here I am my dear, it is I, your loving prince. You have waited a long time." What's this? She doesn't want to be rescued. Can you believe that? She tells me to go back to my purposeless monotony. Who does she think she's talking to? *(Turns to Alexandra.)* Who do you think you're talking to? I don't want to be the one to tell you, you must be outta your fucking mind. Is there a more befitting slipper princess? *(Turning to audience.)* It's too late for me now. My quest is over. And you know what? *(Turning to Alexandra again.)* I think I liked you better when you didn't have a face. *(Fade.)*

SCENE 10

Joint's Tattoo Joint.

ALEXANDRA: I don't think my decision to want to change is so extreme. *(Pause.)*
JOINT: Why are the cops looking for you?
ALEXANDRA: They're not exactly. The man who is looking for me is a police detective. But… *(Knock at the door. Joint and Alexandra stare at one another a minute. Another knock.)*
COP: Mr. Abaris? *(Alexandra stiffens. More knocking.)* Mr. Abaris, it's Detective Beset.
ALEXANDRA: It's him. Oh God. It's him. *(Joint takes her by the hand and leads her into his bedroom. He opens door. Enter cop. He looks about.)*
JOINT: I could put some coffee on.
COP: I'm not here for coffee, Sir.
JOINT: A tattoo then?
COP: No, I'm here regarding the girl I spoke of yesterday.
JOINT: The girl you spoke of yesterday?
COP: It's a pretty small town, Mr. Abaris. I've been to the general store. I've asked the man at the barbershop.
JOINT: Have you been to the big open space?
COP: I'm wondering if she might have come in here, Mr. Abaris.
JOINT: Call me Joint.
COP: Has she been in here, Mr. Abaris?
JOINT: For a tattoo, you mean?
COP: No. Not for a tattoo.

JOINT: This is a tattoo parlour.

COP: I know that. But she's not that kind of girl.

JOINT: Has she much interest in tattoos?

COP: She has no interest in tattoos. She's a beautiful young woman. Why should she give a damn about tattoos?

JOINT: Why would she come in here then – a tattoo parlour – if not for a tattoo?

COP: That's what I'm going to find out.

JOINT: I'll be straight with you, Sir. You don't get many people coming into your tattoo parlour unless they have some interest in tattoos. It's just the way things are in tattoo parlours. You don't go into a tattoo parlour to get your eyes checked. *(Pause.)* I mean, feel free to look around. There aren't many places to hide. If she was to be anywhere, she'd be right here – in this chair. Quite a comfortable seat, this is. I'd let you try it, but it is only for those about to get a tattoo.

COP: And in there?

JOINT: Small storage room. Real mess. I guess I could be hiding her in there, but... *(Cop makes himself comfortable on the Tattooing Chair. Joint winces.)*

COP: Listen. I've been to the Bed and Breakfast. I've been to the barbershop and I've been to that... stupid Big Open Space. She's not in any of those places. But I know for a fact that she's here in this town. So tell me: what would she want with a blind tattoo artist? *(Pause. Joint falters in step. Lets his blindness show.)* Maybe she has an interest in tattoos after all. *(Pause.)*

JOINT: Are you sure you'll pass on the coffee?

COP: I'm going to find her, Mr. Abaris. She is wanted by the law and I'm going to bring her back with me. If you know where she is, I suggest that you inform me. Otherwise you're guilty too. And I will charge you as an accessory.

JOINT: An accessory to what?

COP: She killed a man, Mr. Abaris. You'll be charged as an accessory to murder. *(Pause.)* I'll be back. Think about it, until then. *(Cop exits.)*

SCENE 11

Alexandra comes out of bedroom, slowly.

JOINT: He thinks you are a murderer. *(Alexandra moves in close to Joint. Intimate.)*
ALEXANDRA *(Whispering):* No.
JOINT: He said you killed a man.
ALEXANDRA: No. Joint.
JOINT: He wants to arrest you for it.
ALEXANDRA: He's not telling the truth.
JOINT: Somebody's not telling the truth. *(Alexandra turns away from Joint, sighing.)*
ALEXANDRA: Peter killed himself. In police custody. They said it was because of a long jail sentence but Peter wasn't going to get a long jail sentence.
JOINT: How do you know that?
ALEXANDRA: Because Detective Beset is Peter's brother.
JOINT: That was Peter's brother?
ALEXANDRA: Yes. And David was going to fix it so that I got blamed for the murders and Peter could go free.
JOINT: David?
ALEXANDRA: Officer Beset. Peter's brother. In his mind I was a cheap harlot who put his brother under a spell.
JOINT: His brother is dead. He still wants you to suffer for it?
ALEXANDRA: Not exactly. He came to my house to arrest me, but when I opened the door the fury fell from his face. He looked pale. "It's you," was all he could mutter. I was tired. I invited him inside. We talked, we apologized. And we... *(Pause.)* ...kissed.

JOINT: Kissed?

ALEXANDRA: Joint, I was scared. Three innocent people had just died because of me. I was afraid he would hurt himself or somebody else. I had to be careful. I was scared Joint. He had that look... and now I'm nothing but a cheap harlot... *(Long pause. Alexandra looks at Joint for a sign of redemption. He gives her none.)* I suppose you want me to go now.

JOINT: Why would I want you to go?

SPEAKING CLOCK: THE TIME IS ELEVEN A.M. ELEVEN IS THE TIME.

SCENE 12

Street scene. Old woman sits alone on bench. She looks left. She looks right. She stares straight ahead. She hangs her head as if asleep. Fade.

SCENE 13

ALEXANDRA: Joint. I want to show you... I want you to see me.
JOINT: I thought the whole purpose was that I wasn't able to see you.
ALEXANDRA: I want you to. I trust you.
JOINT: Why do you trust me?
ALEXANDRA: Because you see things differently. *(Alexandra takes Joint's hands and places them softly on her face. Joint does the rest, moving his middle fingers softly along her hairline, pausing on the outline of her jaw, moving to her cheeks and up to her forehead. His fingers wash down over her eyes and nose and rest momentarily on her lips. His hands continue to wash down her neck, chest, abdomen. Finally, Joint's hands drop to his side and he "stares" at the ground.)* I want everybody to see me the way that you see me. *(Long Pause.)* Joint? *(Long Pause.)* And then more desperate... Joint? Joint? *(Pause.)* Joint walks over to tattoo table.
JOINT: Beauty resides in proper measure and proper size of parts that fit.
ALEXANDRA *(Instinctly):* What?
JOINT: That is how Plato defined beauty. And in doing so, he provided our society with a standard. A standard against which we may measure objects for their individual quality of beauty. It's what we now call idealism. *(Pause. Alexandra doesn't get it.)* It's the reason you're here. You're a victim. *(Alexandra moves closer to Joint. He*

reaches out and touches her face. He pulls her in as if to kiss her. Suddenly, Alexandra pulls away from him.)

ALEXANDRA: Wait! Does this mean you can do it? You'll do it?

JOINT: I'll just disrupt Plato's Ideal. All I need to do is upset the proper measure of your most significant feature. *(Joint touches her face.)* Just slightly. And all the other parts, won't fit. *(Pause.)* It'll take some time.

ALEXANDRA: Can we do it then? Can we get started? *(Pause.)*

JOINT: Before anything happens, I gotta warn you. I can make the actual work... the actual tattoo... quite subtle. You'd hardly even notice it. But the change, the actual change will be drastic.

ALEXANDRA: I want drastic. Drastic is what I've been waiting for.

JOINT: And it'll hurt. *(Alexandra laughs. Joint turns the tattooing chair just so.)*

SPEAKING CLOCK: THE TIME IS ELEVEN-FIFTEEN A.M. ELEVEN-FIFTEEN IS THE TIME. *(Fade out.)*

SCENE 14

Fade in. Alexandra sits in chair, with back to audience. Joint takes a step back and puts down his tattooing needle. He puts his arms around her and leans into her. Cop comes crashing through the front door. He looks crazed. Alexandra remains seated with her back to him.

COP *(To Joint):* Where is she? *(He spies her and runs to her. Cop puts his hands on her shoulders and spins her around. Pause. He stares at her, mesmerized. He turns to Joint who has now moved to the chair by the large window.)*

COP: Where is she?

ALEXANDRA: David? *(Cop turns in the direction of her voice. Then back to Joint.)*

COP: Where is she?

ALEXANDRA: I'm right here, David. *(Cop pulls gun from his holder and slowly raises it at Joint who is seated and staring out the window.)*

COP: Where is she?

ALEXANDRA: I'm right here.

COP: What have you done with her?

ALEXANDRA: I'm right beside you. *(Cop spins as if hearing voices.)*

COP: Where is she!

ALEXANDRA: David, I'm right beside you.

COP *(To Joint):* Look at me. Look at me, god damn it! *(Cop Moves closer to him, still holding him in sight of the gun. Joint is unaffected, still staring out the window.)* What have you done with her? Where is she?

ALEXANDRA (Shrilly): David, stop! Stop!

COP: Where. Is. She.

ALEXANDRA *(Louder and more abrasively):* David! Don't! Stop! (*Cop turns abruptly turns and shoots in the direction of the voice. Alexandra looks down at her bloody abdomen. She drops, face down. A pool of blood forms.*)

COP: Where is she?

JOINT: I think I just heard her hit the floor. (*Cop looks at her lying face down. The gun falls to his side. He turns to Joint.*)

COP *(Meekly):* You killed her. (*Joint stares on.*) You killed her. (*He moves slowly to Joint, holding him in the sight of the gun, until the gun is right at the back of Joint's head, executioner style.*) Not me. (*Cop's arm falls to his side, limp.*) Not me. (*Then he walks slowly to the door. He exits without a sound. Joint stares on.*)

SPEAKING CLOCK: THE TIME IS NINE P.M. NINE P.M. IS THE TIME. (*Joint moves to the door and flips the sign to "Closed." He walks to where Alexandra is lying. He kneels down before her and turns her slightly. His hands touch her face and his fingers caress the puddle of blood. Joint stands up and walks over to the Tattooing Chair. He sits and removes his sandals. He unbuttons his shirt. He turns the tattooing chair, to face Alexandra's corpse. He retrieves his tattoo needle, sits and puts his bare feet in the pool of blood. His head tilts back. Behind him, lights reveal widow, cop and all other characters, standing silently. Alexandra and others begin to fade into black, leaving Joint alone. He begins to apply tattoo to his own stomach. Buzzing needle into fade out.*)

CURTAIN

Printed in November 2005
at Gauvin Press Ltd., Gatineau, Québec